# *Walking*

## How You Can Be
## An Authentic Christian

# STUDY GUIDE
### For Bible Study
### and Adult Sunday School

# Scott Shannon

# Walking With Jesus

## How YOU Can Be An Authentic Christian

# STUDY GUIDE
### For Small Group Bible Study Or Sunday School

*by*
***Scott Shannon***

# Dedication

To Rev. Jesse Bradley, the pastor of the Sebastopol Community Church and ActivateLife.Org who showed me how to be an authentic Christian. He transformed my life.

Also to my son, Michael, who has helped me in so many ways during my writing of this book.

Once you have purchased this book you may send an email to scott.shannon62@gmail.com to get a link to a downloadable PDF version. Please include a copy of your Amazon purchase receipt in the email. Using this version, you may then print or distribute as many copies as you need to use the book as a study guide. Be sure to view the book "Walking With Jesus: How You Can Be An Authentic Christian" to better use this Study Guide.

# Table of Contents

# How To Use This Book

This Study Guide is intended for use with small group Bible studies, Sunday school classes for those over 16, and for personal reflection as part of your daily prayer.

Based on my own experience with teaching adult Sunday school I recommend the following ideas:

1. Use as many or as few of the "Questions For Discussion" as you choose based on the time you have for the session.

2. Try to get full participation from the group. For example, you can ask for a show of hands from those who want to share their answer to a question. Then, choose from those who didn't volunteer to share their thoughts.

3. As an alternative you may call on members of the group as you please and without a show of hands.

4. To get full participation from the group ask 2-5 people to answer each question.

5. After the group discussion share your own answers to as many questions as you feel are appropriate.

6. When there are scriptural references in a chapter ask different people to read the scripture. Try to choose only good readers if you can. Many people are annoyed by listening to people who are poor readers.

7. Try to keep the discussion light and not overly serious when you feel it is appropriate to do so.

# Walk With Jesus

**Questions For Discussion**

1. What does the phrase, "Walking With Jesus", mean to you?
2. Do you walk with Jesus? How often?

3. What does having a personal relationship with Jesus mean to you?

4. What are the main things you get out of going to church and being a member of a congregation?

5. What is your conception of Hell? Is it a physical place or a spiritual place?

6. Do you know anyone who you think might be going to Hell?

7. What are some of the Gospel truths about salvation?

8. What does repentance mean to you?

**The following words from Jesus are, I believe, one of the most powerful statements He ever made about having a personal relationship with Him.**

**Matthew 7:21-27 -** *Not every one that says unto me, Lord, Lord, shall enter into the kingdom of heaven; but He that does the will of my Father which is in heaven. Many will say to me in that day, Lord, Lord, have we not prophesied in thy name? and in thy name have cast out devils? and in thy name done many wonderful works? And then will I profess unto them, I never knew you: depart from me, ye that work iniquity.*

1. What do you think this scripture means?

2. How may we come to know Jesus as He desires?

The author talks about various types of Christians that we might encounter in our daily lives; Cultural Christians, Carnal Christians, Buffet Christians, and Authentic Christians.

1. What is a Cultural Christian?
2. What is a Carnal Christian?
3. What is a Buffet Christian?
4. What is an Authentic Christian?
5. Which kind of Christian do you want to be?
6. The author states that he believes that the words of Jesus in the Gospels are all that we truly need to learn about salvation and eternal life. Do you agree or disagree with his statement?
7. What other parts of the Bible do you feel are important and why?
8. What does it mean to be more Christ-like?
9. Do you consider this book to be radical, confrontational, or offensive? Why?
10. Do you have any comments that you would like to send to the author? His email address is scott.shannon62@gmail.com.
11. If you know anyone who you feel should get a free copy of his book send the author an email.
12. Did you find any parts of the book difficult to read or accept?

# The Commands of Jesus

This chapter, unlike all of the other chapters, does not contain very much of the author's writing. He listed about fifty or so commands of Jesus in modern English, then followed each command with scriptural references from the Gospels.

1. The author wrote, "It is not enough, as many Christians believe, to be "born again" and to "accept Jesus Christ as my personal savior".

2. What does being "born again" mean to you?

3. What does being an Authentic Christian mean to you?

Let's discuss some of these commandments of Jesus. Note to the facilitator: Refer to your copy of the book and choose one or two scriptural references that you feel best demonstrate the commands and discuss those.

## Love, bless, and pray for your enemies.

**Luke 6:27**
**Matthew 5:43-**

## Preach the Gospel and teach obedience.

**Matthew 28:19**
**Luke 9:60**
**John 21:15-17**

## You must be born again.

**John 3:3-8**

## Follow Jesus.

**Matthew 4:19**
**Matthew 11:28-30**
**Mark 1:17**

John 1:43

John 12:26

John 10:27-29

John 21:22

Matthew 6:9

John 16:23-24

## Don't be distracted from hearing God's Word.

Luke 10:38-42

## Confess Christ before men.

Matthew 10:32-33

Mark 5:19

Mark 8:38

Luke 12:8-9

## Privately rebuke a brother and if he repents forgive Him.

Matthew 18:15

Luke 17:3-4

Don't covet your brother's blessing.

Luke 12:13-15

Luke 15:29-30


# Judge not so that you may not be judged.

Matthew 7:1-5

Luke 6:37

Luke 6:41-42

John 7:24


The laws of the Old Testament, other than the Ten Commandments, do not apply to Christians because Jesus gave us a new covenant. The other laws of the Old Testament were given to the Jews.

Luke 16:16

Hebrews 8:13

Romans 11:27

Galatians 3:13

Hebrews 9:11

Matthew 5:17

Mark 12:30

Matthew 19:18-19

Hebrews 8:6-7

## Love God and others.

Matthew 22:37-40

Mark 12:30-31

Luke 10:25-28

John 15:12

John 13:34-35

## Don't call Jesus "Lord" when you don't obey Him.

Luke 6:46

Matthew 7:21-23

## Don't waste time on argumentative people.

Matthew 7:6

## Pay your taxes and give to God what is His.

Matthew 22:21

Mark 12:17

Luke 20:25

## Don't sell things in God's house.

Mark 11:15-17
John 2:13-16

## Strive for perfection.

Matthew 5:48

## Keep alert and watch for the second coming.

Matthew 24:44
Mark 14:62
Luke 12:35-40
Luke 21:27-28 -

## Do not look with lust at another person or view pornography.

Matthew 5:27-28

## When you pray do it secretly.

Matthew 6:5-6

Do not divorce and marry another, this is adultery. Do not marry a divorced person.

Matthew 5:32
Matthew - 19:9
Mark 10:11-12

Build on the rock of obedience to Jesus.

Matthew 7:24-27
Luke 6:47-49

Quietly do good for God's praise alone.

Matthew 6:1-4
Forgive others.

Matthew 6:12
Matthew 6:14-15
Mark 11:25-26

# Beware of hypocrisy, greed, and the doctrines of men.

Matthew 15:7-9

Matthew 23:28

Luke 6:41-42

Luke 12:1

Luke 20:46-47

# Rejoice when you are persecuted.

Luke 6:22-23

# Be baptized.

Matthew 28:19

Mark 16:16

# Repent of your sins.

Mark 1:15

Luke 13:3-5

Luke 15:7

Luke 15:10

Luke 15:18-24

## Treat others as you would like to be treated.

Matthew 7:12

Luke 6:31 –

## Worship Only God.

Matthew 4:10

Luke 4:8

## Keep asking, seeking, and knocking.

Matthew 7:7-11

Luke 11:9-13

## Have a childlike faith.

Mark 10:15

Luke 18:17

## Invite those in need to eat with you.

Luke 14:13-14

## Don't fear people - fear God.

Matthew 10:28
Matthew 16:23
Luke 12:4-5

## Do not use vain repetitions when praying.

Matthew 6:7-8
Mark 12:40

## Don't call your brother a fool.

Matthew 5:22

## Pay attention to what God will and will not accept from you.

Matthew 12:25-38

## Don't be worried about what you have or don't have.

Matthew 6:25-32

Luke 12:22-30

John 14:1-4

John 16:33

## Honor God with all that you have been given.

Matthew 25:14-31

## Humble yourself and take the lowest position.

Luke 14:8-11

Luke 18:13-14

Matthew 23:12

Matthew 19:30

## Store your riches in heaven not on earth.

Matthew 6:19-21

Matthew 6:33

Luke 12:19-21

Luke 12:31-34

John 12:25

# Do more than expected.

Matthew 5:38-41

# Act with compassion and not prejudice towards others.

Luke 10:30-37

# Believe in Jesus.

Mark 16:16

Luke 9:35

John 12:36

John 6:29

John 20:29

John 14:6

# Live in Me and live in My love.

John 8:31-32

John 15:4

John 15:9

# Don't swear an oath.

Matthew 5:33-37

# Give to those that ask.

Matthew 5:42

Luke 6:30

Luke 6:38

# Minister to others as you would to Jesus Himself.

Matthew 25:34-46

## Questions For Further Discussion

1. Now that we have studied this chapter, how do you define an authentic Christian?

2. What will it mean for you if you don't obey the commands of Jesus?

3. Have you made any changes in your life after reading this chapter?

4. What are some of the "rules" about living a Christian life that are not mentioned here?

5. Should we follow the rules we have been given even though Jesus never mentioned them?

6. Although Jesus has told us to obey the Ten Commandments, what other Old Testament laws has He freed us from?

7. What are some of the Old Testament laws that Buffet Christians like to use against people who do not believe as they do?

8. What are some of the Old Testament laws that Buffet Christians choose to ignore?

# The New Covenant

**Luke 16:16**

**Hebrews 8:13**

**Romans 11:27**

**Galatians 3:13**

**Hebrews 9:11**

**Matthew 5:17**

1. What did the Apostles mean when they said that Jesus had given us a new covenant?

2. What does the author mean by the "doctrines of men"?

**Matthew 22:37**

1. When Jesus made this statement was he saying that we no longer need to follow the other eight commandments from the Old Testament?

2. What are some traditions of the early Christian church that we still follow today?

3. When did these traditions first begin?

4. When did the Protestant Reformation begin, and why?

Note to the facilitator: In case you are not well-versed in history, here is a short answer to the previous question:

The Protestant Reformation began in 1517 when Martin Luther defied the Roman Catholic Church about 95 things he disliked. It received momentum in 1533 when Henry the Eighth, an adulterer and fornicator, wished to rid himself of his first wife, Katherine of Aragon. He couldn't get an annulment or a divorce from the Pope, so He made himself the head of the church in England. He then divorced Katherine and married Anne Bolen.

1. Did you know that there are now 41,400 different denominations in the Christian Church? Why do you suppose there are so many?

2. How does our denomination differ from some other denominations that you are aware of?

3. Why are these differences important?

4. What are your beliefs about evolution?

5. How do your beliefs about evolution have something to do with your salvation, serving God, or your having a personal relationship with Jesus?

6. If you believe that the Holy Bible is the inerrant word of God, then do you obey every law and commandment it contains? Why not?

7. Do you believe that everyone is entitled to their own beliefs even if they are different from yours? Why or why not?

8. Are there sinners in your church?

9. Are you a sinner?

10. Does God view one sin to be greater than another?

11. How could the New Covenant we have with Jesus change the world?

# Prayer

Matthew 21:13

Matthew 21:22

Matthew 23:14

Mark 9:29

Matthew 5:44

*Matthew 6:5-15*

Matthew 26:41

Mark 11:24-26

Mark 13:33

## Luke 21:34-36

1. How often do you pray?

2. How do you feel when you pray?

3. Have you seen people in public making a great show to let everyone know that they are praying?

4. Does God appreciate these kinds of prayer?

5. How may you pray in public so that others are not aware of it.

Note to the facilitator: Now you get a chance to teach, as well as discuss!

Jesus has taught us how to proceed when we pray in Matthew 6:5-15. This does not, of course, mean that we should only say "The Lord's Prayer" when we pray. However, the underlying formula of this prayer is an excellent guide to what our own prayers should be.

Here is an example of how we might use the Lord's Prayer as a guide for any number of prayers. The author used his own prayer practice as an example.

Our Father, Who art in heaven,

Dear Lord, heavenly Father, Friend, beloved God,

Hallowed be thy name,

Praise Him with all of the love that is in your heart.

Thy kingdom come,

Acknowledge His dominion over us all.

They will be done,

Speak of His power and your acceptance of His will.

On earth as it is in heaven.

Again acknowledge His dominion over everything.

Give us this day our daily bread,

Thank Him for providing all of our needs.

And forgive us our trespasses,

Express your sincere and complete repentance for your sins.

**As we forgive those who trespass against us.**

Forgive those who you feel have wronged you in some way.

**And lead us not into temptation,**

Ask the Lord to guide you in living an authentic Christian life.

**But deliver us from evil.**

Ask Him to keep you from further sin. This is also a good place to insert your prayers for others.

**For thine is the kingdom, and the power, and the glory forever.**

Praise Him and thank Him again with your sincere love.

**Amen.**

Amen.

1. Does this seem to you like a good way to pray?
2. How does God feel about rote prayers?

**Four False Beliefs About Prayer**

- **False Belief #1: Prayers Are Requests For Things We Ask Down Here To God Up There.**

- **False Belief #2: If I Pray More Often I Will Get A Faster Response**

1. Do you believe that the more prayers you offer, the faster you will get a response?
2. The author has often heard people say, "I need a lot of prayers." Do you think that more prayers make your need appear more valid to God?

**Matthew 6:7**

- **False Belief #3: Those Who Believe The Most Get More From God.**

- **False Belief #4: God Hears All Prayers But Only Responds To A Christian Prayer.**

# Some Gifts From Jesus

Jesus has given us many gifts, and continues to do so once we have a personal relationship with Him and live as authentic Christians. What are some of the gifts that God has given you?

# Salvation

**Matthew 7:21-23**

1. Why is salvation called a gift from God?
2. What does the author say about salvation?
3. Do you believe he is correct?
4. Are you doing what is necessary for salvation.
5. Is the phrase "Once saved always saved" true?
6. Does this phrase appear in the Bible?

   What does the phrase, "Jesus Christ is my personal savior."

   Mean to you.
7. Do you have an intimate relationship with Jesus every day?
8. Do you repent of your sins every day?
9. Do you praise Him and worship Him every day?
10. Do you resist sin as far as you are able?

11. Do you live a truly Christian life daily, not just on Sunday morning?

12. Do you feel guilt that you can never forgive yourself for?

13. Do you show Christian love to everyone you encounter throughout your day (such as fast-food workers, the garbage man, store employees, a stranger on the street, etc.), or do you only show love to those people that you know?

14. If you cannot do these things then what is holding you back?

15. Do you hold on to a rigid belief about Christianity?

16. Do you insist that all of the doctrine, dogma, and traditions of your church MUST be followed without question or reflection?

# Grace

*John 1:14-17*

"Grace" in the New Testament is the English translation of the Greek word *charis,* meaning "that which brings delight, joy, happiness, or good fortune."

1. Have you experienced this gift from God?
2. How has that affected you?

# Forgiveness

Matthew 6:12-15
Matthew 18:35
Mark 11:25-26
Luke 6:37
Luke 17:3-4

Jesus makes it very clear that we must forgive everybody who we think has wronged us; members of our family, our friends, and everyone else (even the politicians who won't let us have medical care).

1. Are you able to forgive those who wrong you?
2. How has that affected your life?
3. Do other people in your life readily forgive you?

I have seen such wonderful results when one person forgives another. Their anger is gone and there is a new lightness to their being. In my many years of hospital visits I have seen hate that, to me, results in terrible illnesses and suffering.

1. Is there anyone in your life that you have not forgiven?
2. Is there someone in your life that you hate?
3. If so, what is holding you back? Pride, fear, or stubbornness?
4. Do you realize how much your lack of forgiveness is harming your Christian life?

Remember, too, that you cannot have a personal relationship with Jesus if you are refusing to forgive.

# Healing

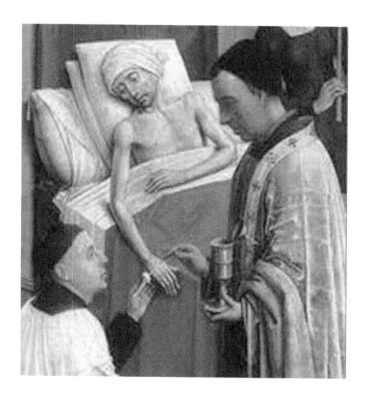

**Matthew 4:23**

**Matthew 9:35**

**Luke 9:6**

**Luke 9:11**

1. Have you ever experienced or witnessed a healing?
2. Why do you think that God would choose not to heal someone?
3. How does prayer assist the healing process?

4. How can you help the healing process?

5. How do you feel about the author's experience of healing?

# Humility

**Luke 14:8-11**

**Luke 18:13-14**

**Matthew 23:12**

**Matthew 19:30**

1. Why is humility needed to be an authentic Christian?
2. Do you think it is right for athletes or award winners to ostentatiously pray in front of their fans?
3. If we want to be humble how, where, and when should we pray?

# Gratitude

**Ephesians 5:20**

**Colossians 3:15**

**Colossians 3:17**

How can we show gratitude to God?

How can we show gratitude to others?

## An Exercise In Showing Gratitude

The author described an exercise in using gratitude to God to gain a new perspective on any problems you may have. Feeling grateful helps you to experience greater love, joy, and blessings in your life. Expressing gratitude to God can help you deal with even the darkest of states.

Is there an area of your life that feels challenging, blocked, or is not going as you want it to.

Is there a problem in your life that is causing you pain, fear, anguish, or frustration?

How can you be asked to feel gratitude for a problem?

Does the situation hold any gifts?

Are there any benefits that you can feel grateful for?

How can this exercise help you?

To help you with this, try asking yourself the questions below:

1. What have I learned from this situation?
2. What gifts have I received from this person or problem that could benefit me?
3. How may my life be better for having to deal with this problem? And if not now, then in the future?
4. Has my love and compassion deepened because of this problem?
5. Have I become stronger or wiser because of this problem?

6. How has this problem helped me to learn more about myself?

7. What good has come from this problem?

8. Has there been any positive inner or outer change in my life?

9. What positive qualities and traits have I demonstrated in dealing with this problem (for which you may feel gratitude)?

10. Can you think of any problems you once had that you are now grateful for?

11. What are you grateful for today?

# Charity

**Matthew 5:42**

**Luke 6:30**

**Luke 6:38**

**Luke 14:13-14**

1. What does Jesus tell us about the poor?
2. How can we best help the poor among us?
3. How do you help the poor?

4. Could you do more to help the poor? How?
5. How can the poor work to get out of poverty?
6. Do state social service agencies adequately meet the needs of the poor?
7. What do you consider to be a living wage?
8. How can restaurants, bakeries, and grocery stores owned by Christians help the poor?

## Matthew 19:21

1. Is it possible to be homeless and poor, and still survive, even with a family in our modern world?
2. Is it possible to follow the spirit and intent of the Matthew 19:21 in our current day and continue to be an Authentic Christian? How?
3. Rather than sell your house, your cars, your clothing, and everything else to live on the street, I believe you may obey this command by moderating your acquisition of possessions.
4. How much do you believe an individual Christian should give to the poor?
5. What are the most pressing needs of the poor?

# Temptation

Why did Satan come to the earth?

Do you believe that Satan has a powerful influence on our world?

How does this show itself?

Do you believe that it is God who sends us temptations?

Why does Satan lead us into temptation?

**How We Might Avoid Temptation**

**James 1:14-15**

How does Satan tempt us to sin?

**1 Corinthians 10:13**

1. Why does God allow Satan to tempt us into sinning?
2. How does God help to save us from sin?
3. What should we do when we are tempted by Satan?

**Hebrews 4:12 -**
**2 Corinthians 10:4-5**

How does the word of God help us resist the temptation to sin?

**Psalms 147:1-7**

Do you find yourself being tempted when you are fully concentrated on our Lord?

- Repent quickly when you fail.

**1 Corinthians 6:18**
**1 Corinthians 10:14**
**2 Timothy 2:22**

**James 1:15**

# Luke_4:8

1. What do these verses tell us about the way to avoid sin?
2. If we continue to sin what will happen to us?

# Worshiping Money

**Matthew 6:24**

1. What does the word "mammon" mean?
2. What is your current relationship with money? How do you spend it? Do you save it? Do you waste it?
3. Do you worship money?
4. What can you realistically do to simplify your life?

5. Do you have more cars than you actually need?

6. Do you own a boat that you rarely use?

7. Do you have a television in every room of your home?

8. Do you wear expensive suits or dresses?

9. Do you need an expensive car?

10. Do you need more than one house?

11. Do you need the most expensive cuts of meat on your table?

12. How often do you go shopping?

13. Do you have too much debt? Why?

# Love, Marriage, and Sex

This chapter of the book deals with matters that may be difficult for some people to deal with. I recommend that you not require anyone to answer a question that they do not wish to answer. Before the discussion tell them, "If you are not comfortable answering a question, we understand. If you are called upon and don't wish to give a response just say, 'I'd rather not answer that'. That will be perfectly acceptable."

Luke 20:34
Matthew 19:

**Luke 16:18**

1. What did Jesus say about marriage?
2. What did Jesus say about divorce?
3. What is fornication?
4. Why do you think that our culture accepts millions of fornicators?
5. When do you think the current epidemic of fornication began in our country?

An Epidemic of Adultery

Matthew 5:27-28
Matthew 5:32
Matthew 19:9
Mark 10:11

1. What did Jesus say about adultery?
2. Did Jesus say, say "Do not commit adultery unless your church says it is alright"?
3. Are people who are divorced and remarried committing adultery according to Jesus?
4. How do you feel our church should deal with people who are divorced and remarried?
5. How does the Roman Catholic Church deal with divorced people?

# Some Behaviors That Can Destroy A Marriage

## 1st Corinthians 13:11

There are so many factors that can work against having a good marriage. The author lists ten of the biggest threats to a marriage that every couple should be on the lookout for. Ask members of the group to choose and discuss a threat.

1. Failure To Put Your Family Before the Demands of Others.

2. A Lack of Communication.

3. Failure To Deal With Stress Effectively.

4. Allowing Technology To Interfere With Your Time.

5. Being Selfish.

6. Refusing To Forgive.

7. Having Poor Boundaries.

8. Not Letting Go of the Past.

9. Being Dishonest.

10. Bringing Violence Into Your Marriage.

## Disciplining Your Child Without Violence

1. Is the old saying, "Spare the rod and spoil the child", in the Bible?

2. What are you teaching a child when you spank, whip, or beat him?

3. How would you feel if you were treated this way by other people in your life?

4. Can physical punishment lead to child abuse? How?

5. Do you use time-outs to discipline your child?

6. Are traditional time-outs effective?

7. What is an "Active" time-out?

8. Do you think an active time-out might be more

effective than a traditional time-out? Why?

9. What is an alternative to using physical punishment or a time-out?
10. What are logical consequences?
11. Have you used logical consequences as a method of disciplining your child?
12. How would you discipline your child if physical punishment was against the law?

# How Do You Know That You Are In Love?

How did you learn about love?

What kind of messages does the media give us about love?

The author gives us a number of tests we can use to ensure that we are in love.

1. Have you used any of these tests when evaluating your own relationships?
2. Which ones?
3. What did that teach you?
4. Have you ever terminated a relationship because it didn't meet the tests of love?

- **Time**
- **Focus**

- **Knowledge**
- **Exclusivity**
- **Work**
- **Trust**
- **Boundaries**
- **Delayed Gratification**
- **Affection**
- **Physical Attraction**

# The Ideals of Christian Love

## Matthew 22:37-40

The author wrote a poetical version of 1 Corinthians 13:4-8. Did this speak to you in a different way than the scripture? How?

Love suffers long,
and is kind;
Love does not envy;
Love vaunts not itself,
is not puffed up,
Love does not behave itself unseemly,
seeks not her own,
is not easily provoked,
thinks no evil;
Love rejoices not in iniquity,
but rejoices in the truth;
Love bears all things,

believes all things,
hopes all things,
endures all things.
Love never fails.

# The Ideal of Christian Love

## Matthew 5:43-47

The word most used in the Gospels for love are variations of the Greek word "Agápe". (Remember, the Gospels were originally written in Greek.)

1. What does the Greek word "Agápe" mean?
2. Is it possible to show Christian love to EVERYONE we encounter? Why or why not?
3. What are some of the many ways that expressing Christian love for others might affect us?

# The Many Words For Love

NOTE: I believe this section should be taught before it is discussed because we no longer study classical Greek in school. Most people will not be familiar with these words or concepts.

There are a several Greek words that are used to describe love including agápe. The Greek language distinguishes how each word is used. Ancient Greek has four distinct words for love: agápe, éros, philía, and storgē. While only the word Agápe appears in the Gospels, knowing about the other Greek words for love can help us better understand the total human experience of this emotion.

- *Agápe*, as previously discussed, refers to Christian love. This includes both the love God has for us, as well as the love we have for each other.

- *Éros* is physical, passionate love, with sensual desire and longing to become one flesh. It is also an expression of romantic love, which may be pure emotion without the balance of logic. Sometimes *eros* is expressed as "love at first sight". Most teenagers only express this kind of love since their experience and training is limited. *Éros* can also apply to dating relationships, as well as the physical expression of love in marriage.

- *Philia* is "mental" love. It describes an affectionate regard or friendship in both ancient and modern Greek. It includes loyalty to friends, family, and community, and requires virtue, equality, and familiarity.

- *Storge* means "affection" in ancient and modern Greek. It describes a natural affection, like what parents feel for their children and other family members.

# The Marriage Covenant

## Mark 10:8-9

1. What is the Christian Marriage Covenant?
2. What are five vital principles given by the author that make up the Marriage Covenant?

# Marriage and Sex

1. What messages about marriage and sex do we receive from popular culture such as television, movies, web sites, magazines, books, newspapers, and our friends?
2. Is sex God's idea?
3. What messages has god given us about marriage and sex?
4. Is sex supposed to be a pleasurable activity?
5. Is there anything in the Bible that prohibits any kind of sexual expression in marriage?
6. What are some of the tips the author gave for getting the most from your marriage and your sex life?

# Marriage Equality

I have left this chapter out of the study guide because it can be such an explosive issue. I do not wish for Bible study groups and Sunday schools to become areas of conflict and dissension. I hope you understand.

# The Terrible Traditions of The Christian Church

**Matthew 15:9**

**Mark 7:7-8**

1. What do these scriptures tell us about the doctrines or traditions of men?
2. When did the Christian religion begin?
3. When did the laws of men first come into our faith.

**Luke 13:34**

What does this verse tell us about our faith?

Is the Christian religion still like this?

Why do you think the church forbid people from reading the Bible for so many centuries?

Did Jesus preach that there should be an intermediary between us and Him?

Were you taken to other churches when you were growing up?

What was that like for you? What did you learn?

How do those churches differ from our church?

What are some of the rules you were taught that aren't in the Bible?

What does the author mean when he writes about the "Doctrines of Men"?

Can you remember the doctrines of men that you were told about, or may even still be following?

**Tradition**

There are times when tradition may be acceptable or possibly even pleasing to God. But there are certain traditions that may even by hated by Him.

Do any of the traditions of the Christian church violate the commandments of Jesus? Which ones?

**Matthew 15:1-3**
**Matthew 15:7-14**

When was Christmas first practiced by the Christian church?

Does the New Testament tell us to celebrate Christmas?

How did Christmas become a celebration in the Christian church?

Other than because Christmas is an established tradition, is there any reason that we should celebrate it? Why?

Does the celebration of Christmas make God angry? Why or why not?

Is there a way you can honor the birth of Jesus without celebrating Christmas?

What is are some alternatives that the author suggests?

What other Pagan holidays were incorporated into the traditions of the Christian church?

## Matthew 7:21-23

Is there any doubt about how Jesus wants us to follow His teachings?

## Jeremiah 10:1-4

1. Do you recognize the condemnation of the decorated tree centuries before the birth of Jesus?
2. Why would you want to continue this practice now that you know that God condemns it?
3. What are some of the lies that parents tell their children about Christmas and Easter? (If it isn't true it's a lie. "Thou shall not bear false witness...".)
4. How have you felt when you discovered that someone lied to you?
5. Do you think your children might feel this way when they discover the truth about Santa Claus, the Tooth Fairy, and the Easter Bunny?

6. The author believes that it was Satan who seduced the 4<sup>th</sup> century church into including the celebration of Christmas and Easter into the church. Do you agree or disagree? Why?

**John 8:44-47**
**Revelation 22:14-15**
**1 Corinthians 10:20-21**
**Jeremiah 44:19-25**
**John 8:32**

What do these scriptures have to do with holiday celebrations?

**Matthew 6:16**

How does this scripture tell us to behave when fasting?

**John 4:23-24**

1. What does this scripture have to say about truth?
2. If we continue to practice traditions that cannot be pleasing to God, then how can we be considered holy?
3. How are we different or holy as Christians if we continue these Pagan practices?
4. What does the author suggest as an alternative to the practice of Lent or periodic times of fasting?

**Acts 12:1-4**

1. What does the Bible have to say about Easter?
2. How did the feast of Passover begin?
3. Did God say when we should stop practicing Passover?
4. Is Passover still practiced today?

**1 Corinthians 5:7-8**

1. Does the New Testament mention the celebration of Easter?
2. Did the early Christian church celebrate Passover?
3. Passover is honored at a different date each year. How may we find out when it is happening this year?

**Galatians 4:9-10**

The author asks us to consider this story:

It is Spring. We use bunnies and flowers to decorate our home. The parents help the children paint beautiful designs on eggs. The eggs are dyed in many different colors and later placed in special seasonal baskets. Before that we hide the eggs around the home and our children search for them. It's so much fun! The family may also smell the "heavenly" aroma of the hot cross buns that mother is baking in the kitchen. We've been fasting for forty days, but that will stop the next day. Everyone chooses their very best clothing to wear to the next morning's sunrise worship service. This is to celebrate the savior's resurrection and the renewal of life. When we get home from the service we will enjoy a succulent ham with all the wonderful foods that go with it. We'll all have a wonderful day. This is one of the most important religious holidays of the entire year.

Has your family ever celebrated in this way?

Is the story about a modern family?

What did the author say about this story?

## 1 Corinthians 5:7-8

1.  What is Peter referring to in this verse?
2.  What does the author propose as a godly alternative to the celebration of Easter?
3.  What does the following table tell you?
4.  Do you accept these calculations as being accurate? Why or why not?
5.  What does this say about the celebration of Easter by the church?
6.  What do colored eggs, bunnies, and candy have to do with Christ's death and resurrection?

| The Events | | How We Know |
| --- | --- | --- |
| **Nisan 13** | | |
| Jesus and the twelve disciples came into Jerusalem from Bethany, to partake of the Passover meal.

Jesus ate an early-evening Passover meal with His disciples. After the meal, the walks with His disciples towards the Mt. of Olives.

Jesus was betrayed by Judas at the olive grove in Gethsemane, arrested and brought before the high priest, Caiaphas.

The Jewish trial ends at daybreak. | | **Mark 14:12-16** - *And the first day of unleavened bread, when they killed the passover, his disciples said unto him, Where wilt thou that we go and prepare that thou mayest eat the passover? And he sent forth two of his disciples, and saith unto them, Go ye into the city, and there shall meet you a man bearing a pitcher of water: follow him. And wheresoever he shall go in, say ye to the goodman of the house, The Master saith, Where is the guestchamber, where I shall eat the passover with my disciples? And he will shew you a large upper room furnished and prepared: there make ready for us. And his disciples went forth, and came into the city, and found as he had said unto them: and they made ready the passover.* |

| Nisan 14 | | |
|---|---|---|
| In the morning, Jesus was brought before Pilate the governor.<br><br>Jesus was crucified and dies around 3PM<br><br>Jesus' body was placed in the tomb at twilight. | **N**<br>**I**<br>**G**<br>**H**<br>**T**<br><br>**O**<br>**N**<br>**E** | **Luke 23:44-46** - *And it was about the sixth hour, and there was a darkness over all the earth until the ninth hour. And the sun was darkened, and the veil of the temple was rent in the midst. And when Jesus had cried with a loud voice, he said, Father, into thy hands I commend my spirit: and having said thus, he gave up the ghost.*<br><br>This shows that Jesus died around the ninth hour or approximately 3PM. He would have been buried before sunset because of the approaching Sabbath, for that Sabbath day was a high-day.<br><br>**John 19:41-42** - *Now in the place where he was crucified there was a garden; and in the garden a new sepulchre, wherein was never man yet laid. There laid they Jesus therefore because of the Jews' preparation day; for the sepulchre was nigh at hand.* |

| Nisan 15 | | |
|---|---|---|
| This was the first annual Sabbath or high-day - the first day of Unleavened Bread.<br><br>The tomb is guarded and secured by sealing it with a stone. | D<br>A<br>Y<br><br>O<br>N<br>E | **John 19:31** - *The Jews therefore, because it was the preparation, that the bodies should not remain upon the cross on the sabbath day, (for that sabbath day was an high day,) besought Pilate that their legs might be broken, and that they might be taken away.* |
| The annual Sabbath ends at sunset. | N<br>I<br>G<br>H<br>T<br><br>T<br>W<br>O | |
| **Nisan 16** | | |
| With the annual Sabbath now over, the women bought and prepared spices for anointing Jesus' body. | D<br>A<br>Y<br><br>T<br>W<br>O | **Mark 16:1** - *And when the sabbath was past, Mary Magdalene, and Mary the mother of James, and Salome, had bought sweet spices, that they might come and anoint him.* |
| The weekly Sabbath begins at sunset. No work is to be done as commanded in the fourth commandment. | N<br>I<br>G<br>H<br>T<br><br>T<br>H<br>R<br>E<br>E | |

| Nisan 17 | | |
|---|---|---|
| The women brought the prepared spices early in the morning while it was still dark. When they arrived they found that Jesus had already arisen. | D A Y  T H R E E | John 20:1-2 - The first day of the week came Mary Magdalene early, when it was yet dark, unto the sepulchre, and saw the stone taken away from the sepulchre. Then she ran, and came to Simon Peter, and to the other disciple, whom Jesus loved, and said unto them, They have taken away the Lord out of the sepulchre, and we know not where they have laid Him.<br><br>Jesus resurrection had already taken place by the time Mary Magdalene arrived at dawn. And THAT is the day that we celebrate the resurrection of Jesus, whether it falls on a Monday, a Thursday, or even a Sunday, and whether it happens a week before or a week after the "traditional" Pagan celebration of Easter. |

## Ezekiel 8:13-18 –

1. Who is Tammuz?
2. What does the Bible say about worshiping Tammuz?
3. What did Jesus have to say about Satan?
4. Is the celebration of Halloween pleasing to God?
5. What alternatives to the celebration of Halloween did the author propose?

6. Do you think these alternatives will be satisfying for children? Why or why not?

# The Ignorance of
# Many Christians

1. How do some churches welcome or drive away newcomers?
2. How does our church welcome newcomers?
3. Do you think we do enough? If not, what else could we do?
4. Do you have any of the following false beliefs about Christianity?

**Your behavior will affect how God loves you.**

**Church Is Just A Weekly Event That Everyone Attends.**

**Never Express Your Struggles Or Doubts at church.**

**Only The Spiritual Or The Ordained Should Be Part of Church Leadership.**

**The Bible Is Mostly About Rules.**

1. Do you agree with the author that too many Christians are religious illiterates? Why or why not?
2. Do you know any facts about other religions? Why or why not?
3. Can you name the first five books of the Bible?
4. What are the Gospels in the New Testament?
5. What are the four books following the gospels?
6. What do you think about the U.S. Governor who said that, "only Christians should have religious freedom in America."?
7. Do you believe that corporations should be considered to be people?
8. How does a corporation have religious liberty?
9. How is it possible that our Supreme Court could rule that corporations are people with religious liberty?

**Ten Ways Christians Misuse Faith**

Here are some ways that Christianity may be used for the wrong reason:

- As A Form Of Escapism Because You Don't Have Anything Better To Do
- To Get Money
- To Gain Popularity With Your Friends Or Neighbors
- To Avoid Risk and Sacrifice
- To Control Others
- As a Promotional Tool For Your Business
- To Rationalize Bad Behavior
- To Explain the Unexplainable, or to Reject "Secular" Ideas
- Getting The Truth So You Can Put Others In Their Place
- To Change Cultures

1. Have you ever seen anyone practicing Christianity for any of these reasons?
2. How did this make you feel?
3. Do you think it is practicing Christianity when a church hands out guns to encourage attendance?
4. What do you think about some of the things that televangelist Pat Robertson has said?
5. Are these things in line with the teachings of Jesus?

# Christianity and Politics

What did Jesus mean when he said, *"Render to Caesar the things that are Caesar's, and to God the things that are God's."?*

This will be the only discussion question in this chapter. I feel that a discussion of politics and Christianity is not an appropriate subject for a Bible study or Sunday school class. It is not a good idea to be controversial or discuss a subject that can be so charged with emotion. I hope you understand.

# A Special Request From Pastor Scott

If you feel inclined I would appreciate it if you would give an honest review of my book. Reviews help sell books, especially if the reviews are good ones. Bad reviews (one or two-star) at least show that you were interested enough to say something about the book. Three-star reviews usually indicate that you liked my writing, but found some fault in my book's layout or formatting.

If you don't like some or many of my ideas, by all means say so in your review. I want to hear about your views and, as I said in my introduction, you may motivate me to update my book. But please don't give me a bad review unless you <u>also</u> didn't like my writing style (spelling errors, grammar problems, etc.). My book has been proofread and edited professionally by five different people, so I DO want to know about any of those errors you find.

More importantly, it is my hope that my book helps as many people as possible to develop a personal and intimate relationship with Jesus. This is why I offer my book for free on my website, Worldwide-Christian-Ministry Org. Please feel free to direct others to this site if they cannot afford to buy my book. Money is not that important to me because I know that God will provide for all of my needs (not my wants).

If you are not familiar with how to leave a review on Amazon it is really very easy.

- Go to Amazon.com.
- In the search box near the top of the page simply enter my name or the title of the book. If you enter my name you will also see listings for music I have composed, but you will also see the book.
- When you get to the book page scroll down to the bottom until you see a white button labeled, "Write A Customer Review".
- Choose a star rating from one to five (five is best) then write your review (as short or as long as you choose) and submit it.
- That's it! You've done me a great service and I truly appreciate it.

You don't have to be famous, a pastor or priest, or a published author. I want to hear from YOU, an important person to God.

I thank you.

Scott Shannon

Made in the USA
Middletown, DE
02 January 2020